HASTED'S HIS
STAPLEHL

compiled
John W. Brown

LOCAL HISTORY REPRINTS

316 GREEN LANE, STREATHAM, LONDON SW16 3AS

Originally published in 1799 by
W. Bristow of Canterbury. Kent
as part of Volume VIII of
The History and Topographical Survey of the County of Kent
by
Edward Hasted

This edition published in 1997 by
Local History Reprints
316 Green Lane
Streatham
London SW16 3AS

ISBN 1 85699 165 2

INTRODUCTION

Edward Hasted was born on December 31st 1732, the son of Ann and Edward Hasted of Hawley, in Sutton-at-Hone, in east Kent. Edward's father was a wealthy barrister whose family riches had been established by his father, Joseph Hasted (1662-1732), who was Chief Painter to the Royal Navy at Chatham. It was through Joseph's skill in the financial markets that he amassed a large estate that yielded an income of £1,000 a year. The Hasted's came from an ancient Kentish family, branches of which are recorded in Canterbury's registers as far back as 1540.

Between 1740 and 1744 Edward was educated at the King's School in Rochester, after which he spent the following four years at Eton, completing his education with by two years at a private academy in Esher, Surrey. On leaving school in 1750 he briefly followed his father's profession as a lawyer and spent a short period as a member of Lincolns Inn in London.

Edward's father died unexpectedly at the age of 38 and the family subsequently moved to Rome House, near Chatham. In 1752 Edward returned to the old family home at Sutton-at-Hone where, in 1755, he married Anne Dorman, the daughter of a near neighbour. It was at this time that he began gathering the material from which he was to write "The History and Topographical Survey of the County of Kent", the first edition of which was published by Simmons & Kirkby of Canterbury, in four large folio volumes, between 1788 and 1799.

The publication was well received and before the fourth volume was issued Hasted begun work on correcting, revising, and extending the entries in the earlier volumes in order to produce a popular edition of his history in a more convenient octavo size. The smaller volume size meant that the books could be sold at a far cheaper cost than the large tomes of the first edition and hence they appealed to a much wider, general readership. It is from volume VIII of this second edition that this reprint of the entry for the parish of Staplehurst is taken.

The first three volumes of the second edition were published in 1797 by the Canterbury printer, W Bristow. Over the following four years another nine volumes were issued, with the twelfth and final volume being issued in 1801.

Such is the size of the work that Hasted spent the greater part of his adult life involved in gathering material and preparing the text for his history. His research began when he was still a young man in his twenties, and by the time the last volume of the second edition was published in 1801, he was an old man approaching 70. In between he had amassed a wealth of topographical material on the county from sources throughout Kent and London which filled more than 100 bound volumes.

No subsequent history of the County of Kent compares with the sheer size and breadth of content of Hasted's History. The twelve volumes of the second edition contain almost three million words, spread over 7,000 pages, containing an account of every parish in the county. This includes details of the prominent citizens of the area as well as a descent of the various manors and a history of the local church and clergy.

Hasted's achievement is all the greater when one considers the distressing personal circumstances surrounding his life between 1785 and 1807. During this period he left his wife of 30 years for the affections of Mary Jane Town. He was pursued by his creditors and subsequently imprisoned for debt. Following his release in 1802 he lived in poverty in a succession of cheap lodging houses until in 1807, his old friend and patron, the Earl of Radnor, presented him with the Mastership of Lady Hungerford's Hospital at Corsham in Wiltshire.

Edward died at the Master's lodge at Corsham on 14th January 1812 aged 79. His son, the Rev. Edward Hasted, was present at his death and buried his father in the local parish graveyard. In 1929 a monument was erected at Corsham in Hasted's memory by Dr. F. W. Cock of Appledore with the support of the Kent Archaeological Society.

Hasted was a loyal son of Kent and considered his home county to stand "foremost in the rank of all others, so deservedly proud of its pre-eminence in every respect." His History is a fitting testimonial of his love for his county and the fact that no work of similar size and stature has been published since emphasises the magnitude of his achievement.

JOHN W BROWN

HISTORY

AND

TOPOGRAPHICAL SURVEY

OF THE

COUNTY OF KENT.

STAPLEHURST

IS the laſt pariſh to be deſcribed in this hundred, being ſituated the next north-weſt from that of Frittenden. So much of it as is in the north borough, the boroughs of King's Franchiſe and Faircrouch, or Lovehurſt, is in the bailiwic of the Seven Hundreds, and hundred of Cranbrooke ; and another part of it is in the hundred of Marden ; all which above-mentioned is in the lower diviſion of the lath of Scray.

The reſidue of this pariſh is in the lath of Aylesford, viz. that part of it which is in the hundred of Eyhorne, and that part likewiſe called Detling borough, which contains in it ſix or ſeven houſes, is in the hundred of Maidſtone.

The liberty of the court of the bailiwic of the Seven Hundreds claims paramount over that part of this pariſh which is in the hundred of Cranbrooke, ſubordinate to which there are ſeveral ſmall manors, or rather manor farms in it. It is within *the diviſion* of Weſt Kent.

THE PARISH *of Stapleburſt,* though healthy like its neighbourhood, is, excepting the village of it, an unpleaſant ſituation, having a gloomy and dreary appearance ; the country is low, flat, and miry ; the houſes diſperſed at diſtances from each other, and along the broad green ſwerds, and ſmall forſtals in it. The ſtream which comes from Cranbrooke runs along the ſouthern boundary of it, as the Hedcorne ſtream towards

wards

wards Stylebridge does along the eaftern and northern
parts of it. The foil is in general a wet clay, intermixed
with marle at different places, and in the fouthern part
of it fome fand. The high road from Maidftone over
Cockfheath, and by Stylebridge to Cranbrooke and
Tenterden, leads through it, being like the reft of the
high roads in thefe parts fabricated of fand; the bye
roads are equally bad, and nearly impaffable as the
neighbouring ones in wet weather and winter. There
is but very little wood in it.

The village, or ftreet of Staplehurft, is built on each
fide of the great road, at the 47th mile-ftone from
London, being the only part of this parifh which can
be called tolerably pleafant and dry, being fituated on
the fide of a hill, from the knoll of which it continues
to the bottom of it, having the church at the fouth end
of it, and the parfonage-houfe juft below it. The
houfes are moftly old-fafhioned and large timbered;
moft of them fhops, but there are three or four good
modern built houfes interfperfed among them, which
ftand pleafantly on the hill, having a fine view over the
Weald fouthward,

The parifh contains about eighty-eight houfes, and
not quite a thoufand inhabitants. The rents of it are
about 3000l. per annum. There are two meeting-
houfes; one for the Baptifts, the other for the Prefby-
terians.

At the entrance of the village, on the hill, at a fmall
diftance from the high road, on the eaft fide of it, is a
large antient manor-houfe, called *Loddenden*, fituated
within the borough of its own name. It was lately the
property of Mr. Edward Ufborne, deceafed, and now
of his widow, who lives in it.

THE MANOR OF STAPLEHURST was once part of
the poffeffions of the family of Fremingham, or Far-
ningham, as they were ufually called. John, fon of
Ralph de Fremingham, of Lofe, died in the 12th year
of king Henry IV. poffeffed of it, and leaving no iffue,

he

he by will devifed it to certain feoffees, who next year affigned it over, according to the directions of it, to John, fon of Reginald de Pimpe, and his heirs male, with remainder to Roger Ifle, as being neareft of blood to him.

John Pimpe died poffeffed of this manor in the 9th year of king Henry V. and in his defcendants it continued down to Reginald Pimpe, efq. who, about the 12th year of Henry VII. conveyed it by deed to John Ifley, efq. His grandfon Sir Henry Ifley, (whofe lands were *difgavelled* by the act of 2 and 3 Edward VI.) together with his fon William Ifley, being both attainted for the rebellion raifed by Sir Thomas Wyatt, in the 1ft year of queen Mary, their lands and eftates became forfeited to the crown, and Sir Henry was executed at Sevenoke; but this manor ftaid with the crown but a very fmall time, for the queen granted it that year, together with lands here, which had been formerly belonging to the abbey of Boxley, and on the fuppreffion of it had been granted by Henry VIII. to Sir Thomas Wyatt, and come to the crown on his attainder at the time above-mentioned, to Sir John Baker, her attorney general, in whofe defcendants they continued, in a like fucceffion as Siffinghurft, already defcribed, in the adjoining parifh of Cranbrooke, till they were fold in 1752 to Galfridus Mann, efq. whofe fon Sir Horace Mann, bart. is the prefent owner of them.

NEWSTED is *a manor* in this parifh, which was annexed to the free chapel erected here by Hamon de Crevequer, and invefted with feveral privileges; which gift, with all its franchifes, was confirmed to it in the 41ft year of Edward III.[d] But this chapel, with all others of the like fort, being fuppreffed, and their revenues given to the crown, by the act paffed anno 1 Edward VI the king, not long afterwards, granted this

---

[d] See the firft book of compofition kept in the Regifter's office at Rochefter.

manor

manor to Sir Edward Wotton, knt. one of his privy-council, in whofe defcendants it continued down to Thomas, lord Wotton, who died in 1630, and before his death had fettled it in marriage upon his eldeft daughter and coheir married to Henry, lord Stanhope, fon and heir of Philip, earl of Chefterfield. After which, fhe, by her feoffees in truft, paffed it away to Mr. Robert Oliver, of Leyborne, whofe fon, of the fame name, leaving an only daughter and heir Juliana, fhe carried it in marriage to Edward Covert, efq. of Suffex, who likewife left one daughter and heir, and fhe marrying Mr. Henry Saxby, entitled him to it. Soon after which it was alienated to Hales, and Mr. James Hales, of Rochefter, in 1730, conveyed it by fale to Mr. Thomas Mercer, of Hawkhurft, whofe fon Mr. William Mercer died poffeffed of it fome few years ago, and his fon John Dunmoll Mercer, now of Hawkhurft, is the prefent owner of it.

This eftate confifts of two farms, adjoining to each other, called *Great* and *Little Newfted*, the latter of which claims an exemption of tithes. On this farm are the remains of a moat, and there is fome appearance of a building having antiently ftood within it.

There has not been any court held for it for many years.

HENHURST, as it is now called, was in antient times known more properly by the name of *Engehurft*, as appeared by fome old datelefs deeds relating to the bounds of fome lands in this parifh, in which they were mentioned to be fituated *juxta terras Ofberti de Henghurft fupra dennam de Enghurft*, and from this denne did that antient family of Enghurft, or Henhurft, take the firft origin of its name, bearing for their arms, as appeared by feveral feals, for their paternal coat, *Barry, of fix pieces*; and having continued in poffeffion of this place from the reign of Edward II. till that of Henry VI. at length Henry Henghurft, in the 23d year of it, fettled it, by his feoffees in truft, on his kinfman John Nafh,

in

in which name it continued in the reign of Henry VII. and was then alienated to Sir William Kempe, of Ollantigh, sheriff anno 20 Henry VIII. and he died possessed of it at the latter end of that reign. His son Sir Thomas Kempe, alienated it to Thomas Roberts, who held it of the manor of West-court, in Detling, and died possessed of it anno 5 and 6 Philip and Mary. At length one of his descendants John Roberts, alienated it to Henry Moody, who died before the middle of king James I.'s reign, and left an only daughter Sybell, who carried the manor of Henhurst in marriage to Thomas Lusher, who, before 1634, had alienated it to Samuel Hovenden, gent. who bore for his arms, *Chequy, argent, and sable, on a bend, gules, three lions heads erased, or,* and died soon after the death of king Charles I. by one of whose daughters and coheirs Elizabeth, it was carried in marriage to Patrick Tyndall, gent. whose son Thomas was possessed of it at the latter end of the reign of Charles II.ᵉ His heirs alienated it to Mr. John Love, whose grandson leaving an only daughter and heir, she entitled her husband Mr. John Waller to the possession of it; but the remainder, on failure of issue by them, is vested in her kinsman Mr. John Love, of this place.

SPILSILL-COURT was once, as appears by antient deeds, the residence of a family of that name, who, before the end of king Edward II.'s reign, were extinct here, and it was become the property of Stangrave, of Stangrave, in Eatonbridge; for Sir Robert de Stangrave, at his decease in the 12th year of Edward III. held some estate at Spilsill, but about the end of that reign the Maineys were become owners of it; in which name it continued down to Walter Mayney, second son of John Mayney, esq. of Biddenden, who kept his shrievalty here in the 13th year of queen Eli-

* The above account is entirely taken from the court-rolls of West-court manor.

zabeth.

zabeth.[f] His defcendant, in the reign of king James I. fold it to Mr. John Sharpye, clothier, who refided here, and died in 1613. His fon, of the fame name, who died in 1617, left an only daughter Frances, married to Mr. George Thomfon, of London, in whofe right he became poffeffed of it; and in his defcendants it continued till it was fold to Nicholas Toke, of Maidftone, by whofe daughter Conftance it went in marriage to Mr. William Ufborne, gent. of this parifh, defcended of anceftors of long ftanding in thefe parts, who bore for their arms, *Quarterly, firft, and fourth, ermine, of five fpots; fecond and third, azure, a crofs, or;*[t] and his fon Nicholas Toke Ufborne, gent. now of Staplehurft, is the prefent owner of this eftate.

AYDHURST, ufually called *Little Aydhurft*, is a manor here, lying about three quarters of a mile north-weft from the church, the manfion of which has been fome time gone to ruin. It was formerly the property of the family of Lambe, of Sutton Valence, one of whom, Thomas Lambe, gent. poffeffed it in 1692, whofe daughter and heir carried it in marriage to Thomas Peene, junior, and he fold it to Jeremy Parker, whofe defcendant Auguftine Parker, in 1752, paffed it away by fale to Mr. John Rawlins, of Maidftone, whofe widow Mrs. Rawlins, at her deceafe within thefe few years devifed it by her laft will to Mr. George Prentice, timber-merchant, of that place, who is the prefent poffeffor of it.

There is no court held for this manor, which is held of that of Sutton Valence, and is defcribed in the rolls by the name of *part of the denne of Adhurft*.

WIDHURST, alias LOWER PAGEHURST, by which latter name it is ufually called, is a manor, fituated at a very fmall diftance fouthweft from that laft defcribed.

[f] Viftn. co. Kent, anno 1574. Pedigree Mayney.
[t] Pedigree of this family in the hands of Mr. Ufborne, beginning in 1405

It

It was fometime fince owned by Mayo, who devifed it by will to Mary his wife, for her life, and fhe having remarried Mr. John Philcocks, entitled him to it for that time, but on her deceafe it became divided in fhares among her feveral children, and they are now refpectively entitled to it. A court baron is held for this manor.

LOVEHURST is a manor, which lies about a mile and a quarter fouthward from Lower Pagehurft, and is of fomewhat more confiderable account than thofe laft mentioned, giving name to a fmall borough in this hundred. This manor was given among other premifes, in the reign of Henry II. by Robert de Thurnham, by the defcription of all his land at Lofherfte, with its appurtenances, to the priory of Combwell, in Goudhurft, at that time founded by him,[a] and it remained part of the poffeffions of it till the 27th year of Henry VIII. when it was fuppreffed by the act then paffed, as not having revenues to the clear yearly value of two hundred pounds.

This manor remained but a fmall time in the crown, for the king, in his 29th year, granted it to Thomas Culpeper, gent. to hold *in capite* by knight's fervice; but he did not continue poffeffed of it long, for it appears by the efcheat-rolls, that it was again in the crown in the 34th year of that reign, when the king granted this manor, with its appurtenances, to Sir John Gage, to hold in like manner. He fold it to Thomas Wilsford, efq. of Hartridge, whofe fon, of the fame name, had poffeffion granted of it in the 7th year of queen Elizabeth. Soon after which he alienated it to Mr. John Baker, from which name it paffed in that fame reign, to Stanley; at length, after fome intermediate owners, it came into the name of Johnfon, one of which, about fifty years ago, gave it by

[a] See the confirmations of it in Dugd. Mon. vol. ii. p. 270.

will

will to St. Bartholomew's hofpital, in London, part of the revenues of which it continues at this time.

The borough of Lovehurft has a court leet of itfelf, holden at the manor of Lovehurft, and the inhabit-ants of it owe no fervice to the court leet for the hun-dred of Cranbrooke ; but at this court leet of Love-hurft, a conftable for that hundred may be chofen out of this borough.

AT A SMALL DISTANCE from the fouth end of the village of Staplehurft is *Iden-green*, on which ftood, till within thefe few years, the manfion of THE MA-NOR OF IDEN. This manor was formerly the pro-perty of Chiffinch, from one of which name it paffed to Brian Fauffett, efq. of Heppington, whofe fon the Rev. Mr. Bryan Fauffett fold it, about twenty years ago, to Mr. Thomas Simmons, gent. the prefent owner of it.

There was a court held for this manor about feventy years ago, on Iden-green, under an oak, and fome years afterwards in the manfion ; but the oak being felled, and the houfe taken down, none has been held fince, nor probably will be again.

MAPLEHURST and EXHURST, are *two manors* here, which in ancient times were of no fmall account, the former of them being fituated within the bounds of one of thofe thirteen denberries which Kenewulf, king of Mercia, and Cuthred, king of Kent, gave to Wernod, abbot of St. Auguftine's, Canterbury, at the time he gave to that monaftery the manor of Lenham, being called in that grant *Mapulterhurft*. This eftate was in the reign of Edward I. in the pof-feffion of the family of St. Leger, and Thomas de St. Leger, in the 29th year of that reign, had a grant of *free warren* for his lands at Mapelherft ;[1] and in his defcendants it continued till it was at length fold to Roberts, or Robefart, one of which name, Sir Lewis

[1] Rot. Cart. ejus an. N. 15.

Robefart,

Robefart, died poffeffed of it in the 10th year of king Henry VI. How long it continued in that name, or who were the fucceffive owners of it from that time, I have not found; but in later times they both became the property of Speke, one of whom, in 1720, fold them to David Papillon, efq. of Acrife, in this county, whofe fon David Papillon, efq. late of that place, is the prefent owner of it.

CHARITIES.

LANCELOT BATHURST gave by will in 1639, 150l. for the fupport of a fchoolmafter, to inftruct the fons of the poor in reading, writing, and accounts, which, with 40l. raifed by the contribution of the parifhioners, purchafed a farm, rented at 10l. per annum, which the fchoolmafter receives, and is obliged to teach ten boys for it.

MAJOR JOHN GIBBON, who was born and baptifed in this parifh, gave by will in 1707, the remaining term in three Exchequer annuities of 70l. value (after the death of three relations) to the churchwardens and overfeers of this parifh, for the educating of poor boys in reading, writing, and arithmetic, and binding them apprentices to handicrafts and other trades. Philips Gibbon, efq. furvivor of the three, dying in 1762, there were then forty-two years to come unexpired, which being fold, by virtue of a decree in chancery, and the money laid out in the purchafe of three per cent. confolidated annuities, produced a dividend of 50l. per annum, which is applied by the truftees appointed by the faid court, according to the teftator's intention.

THIS PARISH is within the ECCLESIASTICAL JURISDICTION of the *diocefe* of Canterbury, and *deanry* of Sutton.

The church is dedicated to All Saints. It is a large handfome building, confifting of two ifles and two chancels, having a tower fteeple, with a beacon turret at the weft end, in which are five bells. On the outfide of the fteeple, over the weft door, is a coat of arms, viz. *A lion, rampant*; on the right fide another coat, impaled, but defaced; on the left, one, being *a crofs, engrailed*, over a dormant window on the roof, on the fouth fide in the church, is a curious antient canopy or ceiling of woodwork, in fquare compartments,

ments, on which are carved defigns of fheers, fuch as are ufed by clothiers, and a crown, and a portcullis, &c. By the emblem of the fheers, it is fuppofed to have been put up by fome one exercifing that trade. The fouth chancel is faid to have belonged to Spilfill court, there is a tomb of Betherfden marble in it, on which were the figures of a man between his two wives, that on the left hand only remains; it probably belonged to one of the family of Mayney. In the church-yard are feveral tomb ftones for the family of Love, moft of the infcriptions of which are obliterated, and one for Edward Simmons, obt. 1735.

The earlieft patron I find of this rectory is, John Kempe, bifhop of London, who died anno 4 king Henry VII. poffefied of one acre of land in this parifh, with the advowfon of the church of Staplehurft annexed, held of the king, as of his manor of Marden, as was found by inquifition; and that Thomas Kempe was his kinfman and next heir. He was of Ollantigh, knight, and was the bifhop's nephew, and died poffeffed of it, holding it by the like tenure. His fon, of the fame name, paffed it away to Sir Richard Baker, who was poffeffed of it in 1578, and he foon afterwards fold it to Martin Culpeper, M. D. of Oxford, who, in the beginning of the next reign of king James, alienated it to Robert Newman, S. T. P. in whofe defcendants it continued feveral years; but in the reign of Charles II. John Clayton, efq. was owner of it; at length, about the time of queen Anne's reign, it was fold to the mafter and fellows of St. John's college, Cambridge, part of whofe poffeffions it remains at this time.

It is valued in the king's books at 26l. 5s. 11d. and the yearly tenths at 2l. 12s. 7d. In 1578 there were four hundred and forty communicants here; in 1640, five hundred and eight, when it was valued at 160l. per annum.

There

There is no glebe land belonging to the rectory beſide the ſcite of the houſe, garden, and forſtal in the front of it.

In the Lambeth regiſters are articles of agreement between Robert Newman, clerk, D. D. rector, and his pariſhioners, concerning tithes in 1604; and a further order by archbiſhop Abbot, concerning the ſame, in 1607, in the library there, among the *Cart. Miſcell.*

There are *three farms* in the borough of Lovehurſt, in this pariſh, which pay the rector *a modus* of one ſhilling, in lieu of all tithes.

CHURCH OF STAPLEHURST.

PATRONS, Or by whom preſented.	RECTORS.
	Robert Newman, S. T. B. April 29, 1591, obt. 1612.[k]
Millicent, widow of ſaid R. Newman, pro hac vice.	Robert Browne, A. M. Dec. 30, 1612, ſequeſtered 1642.[l]
	John Sloper, reſigned 1645.
Robert Newman, gent.	Henry Keat, A. M. Dec. 15, 1645.
	Daniel Poyntell, ejected Auguſt, 1662.[m]
John Cleyton, eſq.	Stephen Lowton, A. M. Nov. 7, 1662, obt. 1684.
The Archbiſhop.	Joſeph Crowther, A. M. Aug. 27, 1684, obt. 1719.
Maſter, &c. of St. John's college, Cambridge.	John Bowtell, S. T. P. Dec. 22, 1719, obt. 1752.[n]
	Michael Burton, D. D. March 2, 1754, obt. March 3, 1759.
	John Taylor, S. T. P. Aug. 20, 1759, obt. Dec. 29, 1784.
	Thomas Thompſon, A. M. 1785 obt. 1786.[o]
	Henry Grove, A. M. 1786, the preſent rector.

[k] His will is in the Prerog. office, Cant. It appears by it, that he was of New College, Oxford, to the fellows of which ſociety, preaching at St. Paul's Croſs, London, he bequeathed 10l. per annum for ever.

[l] Walk. Suff. Clerg. pt. ii. p. 203.

[m] Calamy's Life of Baxter, p. 286. Kennet's Chron.

[n] Fellow of St. John's college, and vicar of Patrixtborne.

[o] Head-maſter of the king's ſchool at Rocheſter, and vicar of Hoo.

APPENDIX.

CONTAINING

ADDITIONS AND CORRECTIONS,

TO THE

SEVENTH AND EIGHTH VOLUMES.

TO VOLUME VII.

STAPLEHURST.

PAGE 120, *laſt line but* 5 *from the bottom. Loddenden* Mr. Nicholas Toke Uſborne now owns and reſides in it.

PAGE 123, *line* 24. HENHURST now belongs to Mr. Thomas Watſon, ſurgeon, of Staplehurſt.

PAGE 124, *laſt line but* 4 *from the bottom.* Mr. George Prentice is dead, and his heirs now poſſeſs it.

PAGE 125, *line* 6. LOWER PAGEHURST is now come into the poſſeſſion of Mr. Stephen Walter and Mr. John Am-hurſt, both of Marden.

PAGE 126, *line* 17. IDEN has ſince become veſted in Mr. John Simmons and Mr. William Spong, both of Sta-plehurſt, who now own it.

PAGE 127, *line* 8. MAPLEHURST is now become the property by ſale of Mr. William Spong above-mentioned, of Staplehurſt, who lives at it, and EXHURST belongs to the Rev. Harry Grove, rector of this pariſh.